C000176232

Steam City
CARLISLE

By Howard Routledge

Irwell Press Ltd

Copyright IRWELL PRESS LIMITED
ISBN-10 1-903266-82-3
ISBN-13 978-1-903266-82-3

First published in the United Kingdom in 2007
by Irwell Press Limited, 59A, High Street, Clophill,
Bedfordshire MK45 4BE
Printed by Konway Printhouse.

II

Contents

After traversing the Settle-Carlisle line, Leeds Holbeck based Stanier Jubilee No.45697 *Achilles* completes the short climb into the Citadel station with a Glasgow bound express in July 1966. The Black Five in the distance is being held by signals on the west coast main line, waiting for a platform to become available. This was a common sight on summer Saturdays, and on certain holiday weekends, such as Glasgow Fair, a number of trains could be queuing at signals waiting for access to the station. Howard Routledge.

Author's Introduction

The history of Carlisle as a major railway centre has been well documented over the years, the seven different railway companies that served the city prior to the 1923 Grouping leaving a legacy that lasted well into the 1960s. This book, although not intended to give an historical account of the subject, provides a photographic record from 1951 until the demise of steam operations in the city on 31st December 1967. It also includes a look at two of the lines with summits most associated with Carlisle, Shap and Ais Gill, both of which saw steam activities end on the same date.

For a young steam enthusiast, Carlisle was a magical place to live during this period. Although not a big city, it was certainly a major rail centre that had a vast and varied allocation of steam locomotives on its books. In addition to this, it provided the unique opportunity to see former LMS Pacifics working alongside those from the LNER. As well as 'Princess Royal' and 'Coronation' class locomotives handling principal expresses such as the *Royal Scot*, *Mid-day Scot* and *Caledonian*, former LNER locomotives were working into the city on passenger and freight workings from Edinburgh and Newcastle. At the other end of the scale, pre-grouping locomotives were still running around Carlisle, albeit on local services.

Even by the turn of 1960, Carlisle still had three major steam depots and the majority of trains, passenger as well as goods, were still steam hauled. Although diesel multiple units had appeared on certain local services by the latter part of the 1950s, this failed to detract from the colour and variety that the steam era offered, a situation that was unparalleled anywhere else on the railway network.

Freight workings within Carlisle were intensive and far from straightforward, with no fewer than seven yards (all dating from pre-grouping days) receiving trains as they entered the city, either north or south. The operators were then faced with forming transfer freights to be tripped to other yards within the city, where they were marshalled once more, ready for despatch to other parts of the country. Each engine shed supplied locomotives for these yard to yard trip workings which added greatly to the bottleneck conditions which sometimes prevailed, even though Carlisle had a system of goods lines which avoided the Citadel station. As if this wasn't enough of a headache for the authorities, locomotives were at regular intervals running to or backing down from all three sheds to Citadel. On arrival, ready to take a train, they would sit patiently on one of the spare roads in order to complete a locomotive changeover with an incoming express. Considering that the station had only three through platforms, one can now imagine the intensity of steam locomotive

Upperby based Stanier Coronation class Pacific No.46238 *City of Carlisle* at Carlisle Citadel station on 15th February 1964 with one of three steam hauled football specials ran to Preston that day. Howard Routledge.

movements throughout the city especially during peak periods.

The three surviving steam Motive Power Depots, Kingmoor, Upperby and Canal, were the main attraction for visiting enthusiasts. A visit to all three on any Sunday could bring a bag of nearly 200 locomotives on shed. Kingmoor was the biggest, a large eight road depot situated beside the west coast main line to the north of the city; Upperby was similarly situated but to the south. Upperby had the glamour, for nearly every example of former LMS passenger classes could be seen stabled there within the light and airy modern roundhouse, whilst Kingmoor in appearance seemed to recall something of an earlier era.

The smallest shed was Canal which lay to the north-west, between the Waverley line and the Silloth branch. This housed mainly former LNER class locomotives that were employed on the Newcastle and Edinburgh lines, and in addition to Gresley Pacifics, former North British locomotives dating from before the Grouping were still much in evidence at the end of the 1950s.

The change from normal steam operations really got underway during 1961 when the principal express passenger trains passed from steam to diesel haulage. The days of seeing a 'Coronation' Pacific rolling into Citadel station, sporting a tartan 'Royal Scot' headboard at the head of the Region's premier express, were certainly numbered. All passenger workings on the Waverley line, with the exception of local trains, were likewise changed to the more modern form of traction. The year would also witness a changing scene on the freight side as work was nearing completion on the new marshalling yard north of Kingmoor. This obviously led to the closure of the former pre-grouping yards, and brought to an end the yard transfer trip workings and a lot of the pre-grouping engines that worked them.

As the decade progressed, further changes were witnessed with the increasing use of diesel locomotives on passenger trains, but the freight side remained predominantly in the hands of steam. The Canal depot closed during 1963 and 1964 saw the end of the LMS Pacifics with the mass withdrawal of the remaining 'Coronations'.

As the run-down continued, steam locomotives were increasingly looking the worse for wear and were usually running in an unkempt condition at best. Locomotives that once sported nameplates that had unwittingly provided such a comprehensive and varied history and geography lesson, were now bereft of them. By 1965 the colour and variety was all but gone. This sorry state of affairs finally came to an end in the city on 31st December 1967 with the closure of Kingmoor MPD; the steam locomotive in everyday service was no more.

My interest in steam locomotives began as a youngster in the late 1950s, assisted no doubt by occasional visits to Citadel station accompanying my father in the course of his employment. The

hustle and bustle of a busy environment plus the sight of those huge steam locomotives, many with names to fire the youthful imagination, certainly left its mark.

During the early part of the 1960s a number of us living in the city began to meet at the lineside, a favoured spot being the parkland behind No.3 signal box on the west coast main line north of the Citadel station. From there, goods and passenger workings could be observed in between games of football or cricket.

Some of the group were into their final years of school whilst others had started to be gainfully employed, a number with British Railways. As finances improved with the change from school to work, cameras were purchased in order to record steam workings within the city and beyond. Schoolboy days with the family Kodak Box Brownie gave way to 35mm

cameras as attempts were made to emulate the work regularly seen in magazines such as *Trains Illustrated,* by icons like Canon Eric Treacy and others. A camera favoured by some was the Ilford Sportsman, whilst others, including myself, acquired a Halina 35x. These cameras were extremely basic mechanical types with a fixed lens, and in the case of the Halina, a top shutter speed of 1/200th of a second was expected to stop even the fastest of the expresses. It is extremely doubtful if even that top speed was achieved by a mechanical process, but the situation was further compounded by the lack of an exposure meter. With this part of the procedure having to be guessed at, a grasp of photographic matters had to be quickly attained.

Present day photographers with modern automatic cameras would be

amazed at the basic quality of photographic equipment that was used to record a large number of photographs contained in this book. Some of the photographers, moreover, were still in their teens.

Black and white photography was still the order of the day but as the decade progressed one or two began experimenting with the more expensive medium of colour. I remained faithful to monochrome using mainly Ilford FP3 and HP3 which I would take to the offices of the *Carlisle Journal* newspaper to be developed.

Those were indeed magical days but by late 1966 I'd had seen enough of the decline of the steam scene and the interest waned to the point that I took very few photographs after that time. Others also began to drift into other interests and a way of life which had kept us occupied for years was over for some of us, even before the official end of steam workings in the city.

The idea for this book originated several years ago, a book on the Carlisle steam era with the photographs, hopefully, having been taken in the main by local photographers. From the 1960s group, no fewer than five of us still had negatives or transparencies that I could work from, but it became apparent that this was not to provide enough of the variety that I was looking for. My years working with preserved steam on the main line led to contacts with railwaymen and photographers who had material to more than fill this void. Although the number of contributors has increased during the period I have spent collating material for the book, no fewer than thirteen originate from the Carlisle area, whilst another two were regular visitors to families residing in the locality.

I am extremely indebted to all of the photographers who have generously allowed me access to their collections and to numerous former railwaymen who have given detailed information on the workings of the railway in the Carlisle area during the days of steam.

Howard Routledge
Carlisle
August 2007

A 1908 Reid design for the North British, 0-6-0 No.64511 stands at signals at the north end of Citadel station in August 1952. John L. Alexander.

Former LMS 2P 4-4-0 No.40615 moves down towards the signals at the northern end of platform 4 whilst en route to Kingmoor on 30th June 1951. The imposing buildings above the Victoria Viaduct are still intact to this day but under different use to that shown. Frank Alcock.

The Canal shed had a small allocation of former North British J36 locomotives which were used mainly for yard to yard trip workings within the city. No.65321, minus lamp code, is at the north end of the Citadel station in 1953. A number of photographs in this chapter give a good indication as to the condition of the great glass end screens prior to their removal during 1958. John L. Alexander.

Chapter One
Scenes of Old Citadel

Above. Former North British class D30 No.62428 *The Talisman* arrives at Carlisle during the summer of 1953 with what appears to be an ex-Hawick stopping train. A number of this class, which were named after characters in Scott's novels, were allocated to Hawick, and were daily visitors to Carlisle. John L. Alexander.

Left. Canal C15 No.67481 shunts at the south end of Citadel station, Crown Street Goods depot in the background. The locomotive still has the initials LNER displayed on the tank sides, which is surprising given that the photographer dates the occasion as 5th June 1952, more than three years after the birth of British Railways. J. L. Stevenson, courtesy Hamish Stevenson.

Class D20/2 No.62371 displays an express lamp code as it departs Carlisle with the 3.36pm train to Newcastle during 1952. The D20 class was introduced in 1899, but this particular locomotive was rebuilt with long travel valves in 1936 and re-classified D20/2. John L. Alexander.

Former Midland Railway 3F No.43622, with a 68A Kingmoor shed-plate, acts as the north end station pilot in 1953. The Gresley teak coaches standing in No.7 bay form a train set for Edinburgh Waverley. John L. Alexander.

The Canal shed had four Gresley A3 Pacifics which rarely strayed from the Waverley route. Here we see one of them, No.60068 *Sir Visto* in a reasonably clean condition at the head of a stopping train for Edinburgh, on 28th March 1956. Fellow Canal resident, class B1 No.61064, is running through the station whilst the diesel multiple unit in No.8 bay platform is employed on a Silloth branch train. Frank Alcock.

Thompson class A2/1 No.60510 *Robert the Bruce* backs under Victoria Viaduct whilst en route to Canal shed after having worked a train from Edinburgh over the Waverley route on 22nd May 1956. One of only four members of the sub-class, the locomotive was built at Darlington works in January 1945 but only saw fifteen years service before withdrawal from Haymarket shed in November 1960. The unidentified class A3 Pacific standing in the background adds to the LNER theme. Frank Alcock.

Preston Jubilee No.45633 *Aden* patiently waits to relieve a northbound working, 8th June 1957. J.L. Stevenson, courtesy Hamish Stevenson.

Chapter Two

The Waiting Game

One of the more memorable sights at Carlisle was the line up of locomotives waiting to relieve the engines on incoming passenger workings. This 1953 view shows Coronation class Pacific No.46245 *City of London* ready to detach from a northbound working before retiring to Upperby, whilst Polmadie based classmate No.46230 *Duchess of Buccleuch* prepares to take the train on to Glasgow Central. Standard class No.72005 *Clan Macgregor* waits on a later arrival. John L. Alexander.

The south end of Citadel station in 1953 sees former streamlined Coronation Pacific No.46228 *Duchess of Rutland* moving off in response to the shunting signal at the bottom of the photograph, in order to relieve a Perth to Euston express. The 12A shed-plate refers to Carlisle Upperby at a time when Kingmoor was part of the Scottish Region with the code 68A. What appears to be a Stanier Black Five waits in the background. John L. Alexander.

Upperby based former LMS class 2P No.40629 waits to pilot an up express over Shap on 28th June 1958. Part of a Patriot class smoke deflector is visible on the road behind the 2P whilst Canal B1 No.61239 stands in No.6 bay platform. Martin Welch.

The down 'Royal Scot' appears to be delayed on 29th September 1959 as the driver passes the time checking over his Polmadie Pacific No.46223 *Princess Alice*. David Forsyth, Paul Chancellor collection.

Haymarket A3 No.60090 *Grand Parade* waits to take over the down 'Waverley' express on 18th April 1960. The stock appears to be standing on platform 3, the loosely hanging vacuum brake hose an indicator that a locomotive change is taking place. David Forsyth, Paul Chancellor collection.

A picture that sums up what a summer Saturday in Carlisle was all about. This undated view, probably from about 1960, sees no fewer than five steam locomotives at the north end of Citadel station. Princess Royal Pacific No.46210 *Lady Patricia* has arrived on platform No.1 and has drawn up to a Black 5 still waiting on a signal to clear the station environs. Two Jubilees, 45665 *Lord Rutherford of Nelson,* and an unidentified one paired with a Fowler tender, wait to relieve northbound workings whilst the crews enjoy a breather sitting on the line ahead of the north end station pilot. The photograph also gives a good indication of the work carried out in 1958 to the station; this saw the reduction of the roof area, which included the removal of the ecclesiastical-style glass end screens. Douglas Doherty.

A pair of Kingmoor Clans, 72005 *Clan Macgregor* and 72008 *Clan Macleod*, wait to relieve southbound workings around 1960. The two centre roads at the south end of the station were officially named B and C roads but were referred to by signalmen and station staff as 'Bobby' and 'Charlie'. K. Armstrong.

After arriving at Carlisle, Upperby Britannia No.70036 *Boadicea* with train reporting number 1X10 still up, has already been relieved by Kingmoor classmate No.70054 *Dornoch Firth* on 27th May 1966. 70036 has been allowed to draw up to the rear of a southbound passenger train by means of a 'calling on' signal whilst en route to her home shed. G. Hamsher.

In the mid-1960s efforts to banish the steam locomotive from Britain's railways were redoubled. So it was that by the summer of 1966 the only classes that remained at Carlisle capable of working passenger trains were either Black 5s or Britannias. No fewer than three Black Fives were at the south end of Citadel station on 30th July 1966; No.44892 is preparing for departure with an unidentified express whilst No.44829 and a classmate allocated to Crewe South wait to relieve 1M38 and 1M52 respectively. David Forsyth, Paul Chancellor Collection.

Just to prove the point that there were cleaners employed at Kingmoor, four of them stand on the buffer beam of Britannia 70041 *Sir John Moore* during April 1965. They are (L to R) Joe Hallington, Jack Pattinson, Ian McStephney and Dennis Hastings. 70041 was one of fifteen members of the class to be transferred to Carlisle from the Eastern Region between December 1963 and March 1964. Out of a class of fifty-five engines, no fewer than fifty-one had been allocated to Carlisle at one time or another. G.W. Routledge.

Chapter Three
Kingmoor M.P.D.

The north end of Kingmoor shed with the goods lines and the west coast main lines in the foreground. The two Black Fives, No.45185 and 45061, occupy No.1 road with 9F No.92110 just visible inside the shed. The building had eight through roads and a two road workshop running the full length on the far side. David S. Goodfellow.

A mixture of passenger and freight locomotives occupy the south end at Kingmoor on 13th May 1961. Long-term Kingmoor resident Jubilee No.45732 *Sanspareil* stands alongside Polmadie Britannia No.70051 *Firth of Forth*, whilst Saltley 9F No.92137 buffers-up to an unidentified Hughes mogul. R.S. Greenwood.

Prior to the allocation of 9F 2-10-0s, Kingmoor had a small number of Stanier 8F 2-8-0s on its books, including No.48321, seen here in the company of a former LMS class 4 0-6-0, No.44181 on 1st September 1963. Martin Welch.

A typical shed scene at Kingmoor on 1st September 1963 with Holbeck Jubilee No.45605 *Cyprus* and five Black 5s resting between duties. A visit to the shed on a Sunday, even as late as 1966, could find nearly a hundred steam locomotives present. Martin Welch.

Farnley Junction 8F No.48542, about to cross the west coast main lines at Etterby Junction to gain access to Kingmoor on 4ᵗʰ June 1965. Martin Welch.

The Kingmoor interior with a mix of former LMS and LNER types in April 1965. The concreting of the pit road on the extreme left is undergoing repairs, with the rails removed. G.W. Routledge.

Upperby footplate Inspector Tommy Millican instructs young railwaymen on the Walschaerts valve gear in a classroom at Kingmoor in April 1965. G.W. Routledge.

Jubilee No.45582 *Central Provinces* appears to be in an ex-works condition as it stands outside the rear doors of the two road repair shop during 1957. The 'Not to be Moved' boards relate to the missing tender wheel-set. C. Hill.

An interesting scene inside the workshop on 7th August 1965 sees no fewer than three locomotives under repair with a Black 5 having had its driving wheels removed. The rearmost locomotive is a Clan Pacific. David Forsyth, Paul Chancellor Collection.

On 29th May 1959 the workshop hosts No.72009 *Clan Stewart*, devoid of its left-hand side motion. Although the Clans had a poor reputation on certain parts of the railway, they were considered capable locomotives by a lot of Kingmoor men, especially when used on the 'Port Road' to Stranraer. A small unofficial device lodged in the exhaust to aid steaming might have had something to do with the Kingmoor point of view. R.C. Riley/The Transport Treasury.

The regulator of Stanier Coronation No.46242 *City of Glasgow* is eased open causing the locomotive to slowly inch forward on No.1 road on 13th May 1961. This was one of the three locomotives involved in the 1952 Harrow and Wealdstone disaster. Although the other two engines were condemned, it is open to question as to how much of the original 46242 survived after the extensive re-build. R.S. Greenwood.

Former LMS pacific 46200 *The Princess Royal* at Kingmoor on 23rd April 1962. One of three allocated to the shed at this time, it was the last of the class to be withdrawn from service, during November 1962. Whilst the other two at Kingmoor, 46201 and 46203 survived into preservation, 46200 remained in store at Kingmoor then Upperby until the summer of 1964 before being consigned to the scrap-yard. John L. Bradshaw.

A remarkably clean Kingmoor Pacific, No.46252 *City of Leicester*, makes a fine sight as it turns prior to its next duty, on 13th May 1961. Kingmoor footplate-man Jack Scott is at the turntable control box. R.S. Greenwood.

Above. Princess Royal No.46203 *Princess Margaret Rose* is turned at Kingmoor prior to backing down to Citadel to work a northbound express on 29th August 1962. The figure beyond the tender is none other than Canon Eric Treacey, making full use of his line-side permit. Peter Fitton.

Top right. Adding a dash of colour to the surroundings at Kingmoor on 13th June 1964 is Caledonian Railway 4-2-2 No.123 and Great North of Scotland Railway No.49 *Gordon Highlander*, prior to working a rail tour to Silloth. Peter Fitton.

Right. Newly allocated Jubilee No.45738 *Samson* takes water at Kingmoor on 1st September 1963. It was during this month that no fewer than sixteen Royal Scot class locomotives transferred to Upperby, which in turn moved out all but two of its Jubilees to Kingmoor. Martin Welch.

A number of Kingmoor Jubilees had 3,500 gallon Fowler tenders, as attached to No.45718 *Dreadnought*, backing on to the depot on 13th May 1961. R.S. Greenwood.

Coronation No.46255 *City of Hereford* awaits its next call of duty at Kingmoor on 11th July 1964. David Forsyth, Paul Chancellor collection.

The new order at Kingmoor as a result of the closure of the Canal shed in June 1963. Two former Haymarket Pacifics, A4 No.60024 *Kingfisher* and A3 No.60100 *Spearmint*, both now allocated to St. Margarets and relegated to freights over the Waverley line, are at the former Caledonian stronghold in April 1965. G.W. Routledge.

Class A1 Pacific No.60161 *North British* receives final preparation before leaving Kingmoor to work a goods train to Millerhill yard near Edinburgh on 1st September 1963. Martin Welch.

Above. Polmadie A2 Pacific No.60535 *Hornet's Beauty* prepares to depart Kingmoor on 13th June 1964. An Edinburgh locomotive for many years, it was a regular visitor to the Canal shed prior to the unexpected transfer from St. Margarets to Polmadie in 1963. Peter Fitton.

Top right. George May stands among the tools of his trade as a fire dropper at Kingmoor in April 1965. A3 Pacific No.60100 *Spearmint* is in the final condition for the class, having a double chimney, German style trough smoke deflectors and the yellow cab-side stripe. G.W. Routledge.

Right. Coronation No.46226 *Duchess of Norfolk* in the front yard siding normally used by locomotives awaiting attention in the workshop, or to store those having been withdrawn from service. On 1st September 1963 46226 appears to be waiting workshop attention as it was not withdrawn until the cull of the remaining Coronations during September 1964. It was the last Coronation to leave Carlisle and was still at Upperby in January 1965, weeks after the others had left for the scrap-yard. Martin Welch.

Locomotives arriving at Kingmoor initially went straight to the coal hopper and then onto the ash pit for fire dropping. This April 1965 view sees Crewe North Britannia Pacific No.70010 *Owen Glendower* and an unidentified Royal Scot awaiting disposal prior to being allotted a shed road. G.W. Routledge.

The last Royal Scot to remain in service, 46115 *Scots Guardsman*, has been specially cleaned at Kingmoor prior to its move into preservation at the Keighley & Worth Railway in May 1966. Howard Routledge.

Chapter Four
Upperby M.P.D.

Upperby motive power depot was situated next to the west coast main line to the south of Citadel station. The 32 road concrete roundhouse, built in 1948, housed a large number of former LMS passenger locomotives including several Coronation Pacifics. With the opening of the new yard at Kingmoor in 1962, the adjoining Upperby yard closed and all of the shed's freight work, in addition to a number of footplate staff, transferred to Kingmoor. This view of 13th May 1961 shows a partially smoke obscured roundhouse and a yard predominantly occupied by freight locomotives. R.S. Greenwood.

Three locomotives stand on the shed arrival road awaiting disposal during 1965. The remains of the freight yard can be seen on the extreme left. David Forsyth, Paul Chancellor Collection.

A pair of Upperby Coronations stand on the road outside the roundhouse awaiting their next duties, *circa* 1964. No.46238 *City of Carlisle* stands ahead of 46250 *City of Lichfield*. Although the shed didn't actually allocate a locomotive as a main line stand-by, a Pacific was usually to be found stabled on this line, available in the event of a failure. G. Hamsher.

46256 *Sir William A. Stanier F.R.S.*, stands in front of the Upperby roundhouse on 1st September 1963. This was the last Pacific built by the LMS and also the final one to be withdrawn from traffic in 1964 after a lifespan of only 16 years. The last Coronation to actually enter service, No.46257, did so only after the nationalisation of the railways. Martin Welch.

To the north-east of the depot, two roads ran into an area known as the 'Burma Road', a popular nickname of the period. One of the roads had a pit, brought into use occasionally when the shed yard was particularly busy. David Forsyth, Paul Chancellor Collection.

Taken in 1953, this photograph shows a surprisingly large number of locomotives stabled within the area of the 'Burma Road'; 8F No.48310, Black 5 No.45148 and mogul No.42951. Upon being asked why so many locomotives are seen stabled there, a former Upperby driver, simply replied 'shed full'. John L. Alexander.

Recently transferred from Kingmoor to Upperby, Britannia No.70022 *Tornado* without nameplates stands outside the roundhouse in 1965. After the withdrawal of the Coronations things just didn't seem the same at Upperby. G. Hamsher.

The Black 5 on the left is progressing through the disposal road at Upperby and a brace of Royal Scots prepare for their next duties on 13th July 1963. No.46115 *Scots Guardsman* from Longsight shed in Manchester is to work 1M31, Glasgow-Blackpool, whilst 46165 *The Ranger (12th London Regt.)* carries a 1X76 reporting number. David Forsyth, Paul Chancellor Collection.

The roundhouse had a 70ft turntable and here we see a member of the footplate staff waiting for Ivatt class 2 No.46513 to be correctly positioned before he connects the vacuum pipe to the locomotive on 7th August 1965. David Forsyth, Paul Chancellor Collection.

Former Kingmoor locomotives stored and out of use at Upperby on 1st September 1963. In addition to several of the Hughes moguls, Pacific No.46200 *The Princess Royal* stands ahead of Kingmoor's solitary WD 2-10-0 No.90763. Martin Welch.

One year later and it is the turn of the Coronations to fill the same siding. An accountancy decision in 1964 was the death knell of this class and the eight remaining examples allocated to Carlisle were removed from service on 12th September that year. The author is seen climbing into the cab of No.46250 *City of Lichfield* whilst the former pride of Upperby, No.46238 *City of Carlisle,* stands nearest to the camera. G.W. Routledge.

Chapter Five
Canal M.P.D.

The Canal shed was situated between the Waverley line and the Silloth branch and access was via a wonderfully named roadway called 'Engine Lonning'. Former North British 0-6-0 No.64479 ambles towards Canal Junction signal box with a pick-up freight from Silloth. In the shed yard stands an A3 Pacific, in addition to other locomotives. R. Payne.

Haymarket A3 No.60094 *Colorado* and Canal B1 No.61217 occupy the shed yard on 23rd March 1960. The River Eden flowed past the shed just beyond that sleeper-built boundary. The plume of steam seen in the distance to the rear of the B1's tender indicates the presence of a steam locomotive on the bridge that crossed the Eden near to Etterby Junction at Kingmoor. K. Runton.

The modern looking coal hopper at Canal, on 23rd March 1960. It was not in keeping with the rest of the buildings there, but it certainly put the one at Upperby to shame. K. Runton.

Inside the roundhouse with two Reid-designed former North British locomotives, class J35 No.64499 and class N15 No.69215 on 29th June 1958. Martin Welch.

A further view around the turntable stalls on the same date as the previous photograph shows another N15 tank, No.69155, keeping company with classmate No.69215. The diesel shunter is an ominous presence for the two venerable steam locomotives, built in 1910. Martin Welch.

There was a small yard to the rear of the main shed building with a through line giving access to the wheel-drop shed. The Canal had eleven J39 0-6-0s at the turn of 1960, used on Silloth branch trains as well as local yard to yard trip freights. No.64884 appears prepared for its next duty on 23rd March 1960. K. Runton.

A far cry from days hauling titled trains on the east coast main line. Former LNER class A4 No.60004 *William Whitelaw* occupies the Canal wheel-drop, at the rear of the main shed, about 1960. The coach body on the left served as the joiners' shop. K. Armstrong.

Believe it or not, but this photograph was taken within the confines of the Canal shed and had been set up by the shed staff. Gateshead Gresley A4 Pacific No.60001 *Sir Ronald Matthews* is in the middle of a substantial wheel-slip on a stretch of rail deliberately lubricated with oil. Peter Brock.

Canal A3 No.60068 *Sir Visto* waits to exit the shed to run tender first to Citadel station in order to work a train over the Waverley route to Edinburgh, around 1960. Of the four A3 Pacifics allocated to the Canal, not one of them survived long enough to be fitted with the German style trough deflectors. 60068 was the last one of them to be withdrawn in August 1962. K. Armstrong.

Haymarket A3 No.60096 *Papyrus* stands under the coaling plant at the Canal shed on 13th May 1961. Though obviously not as well known as *Flying Scotsman,* this particular A3 held for a while a world record speed for steam of 108mph attained with a test train on the east coast main line during 1935. R.S. Greenwood.

Chapter Six
Test Trains

During the 1950s, British Railways conducted a number of controlled road tests on the Settle-Carlisle line and on the former Glasgow & South Western line between Carlisle and Hurlford. These maximum power tests involved a number of different classes of locomotives, with additional trials carried out at the Rugby Testing Station. Although the quality of the photograph does not match the photographer's later work, the rarity of the subject alone warrants its inclusion. Southern Region Merchant Navy Pacific No.35022 *Holland-America Line* eases the test train away from Durranhill early in 1952, for evaluation on the steeply graded former Midland line. K. Runton.

Kingmoor supplied the footplate staff for the locomotives on test and this 1954 view shows a group standing in front of a Stanier Black 5 wired for readings. L to R (1) shed staff, (2) Footplate Inspector Joe Armstrong, (3) Driver Willie Kelly, (4) Sandy Willis, Chief Footplate Inspector, Scottish Region, (5) shed staff, (6) Fireman Jim Brodie, and (7) an unidentified guard. Shed staff were employed, *within the tender coalspace* during the test runs moving the measured bags of coal onto the tender shovelling-plate. A safety net was fitted so that they could not accidentally reach beyond the loading gauge. Jim Brodie collection.

Kingmoor footplate staff together with officials from Derby pose in front of Coronation No.46225 *Duchess of Gloucester* which took part in trials during 1956. Hauling simulated train weights up to 900 tons, the locomotive reportedly suffered from heavy bouts of wheel-slip and was the subject of complaints about the damage it was inflicting to tunnel roofs on the Settle-Carlisle line. Jim Brodie collection.

	BRITISH RAILWAYS			OUR REF.	D68A/7/10/55	E.R.O. 11
YOUR REF.	THE RAILWAY EXECUTIVE			DATE	12.12.55.	
DATED						

TO
W. Kelly, Driver, Kingmoor.   REGION
J. Brodie, Fireman, Kingmoor.
E. Elliot, Fireman, Kingmoor.   FROM   Dist. Motive Power Supt.,
                                             Carlisle Kingmoor.
(Centre No.)   Extn._____   (Centre No. 27)

        MOBILE TEST PLANT TRIALS : B.R. FRANCO-CROSTI
        2-10-0 LOCOMOTIVE NO.92023 AND STANDARD B.R.
        9.F 2-10-0 LOCOMOTIVE NO.92050.

        With the conclusion of the series of tests which have been
carried out between Carlisle and Hurlford from October 11th to
December 9th, I would like to take the opportunity of expressing
my appreciation of the work performed by you. These tests have
on the whole been successful and satisfactory although difficulties
were experienced due to failure with the engine or with the dynamo-
meter car, but these could not be attributed to any failure on your
part and I am advised that the satisfactory nature of the tests as
a whole was very largely due to the efficient manner in which the
engine was handled by the footplate staffs.

        While no doubt Mr. Robert has thanked you on behalf of the
Mechanical & Electrical Engineer I would like to take this
opportunity of conveying the thanks of the Motive Power Supt.,
and also my personal appreciation for the very excellant efforts
you made to ensure that the tests were carried out successfully
from a Motive Power point of view.

Copy of British Railways internal memorandums issued to the Kingmoor footplate staff in recognition of their work in connection with the test train involving 9F class locomotive. Jim Brodie collection.

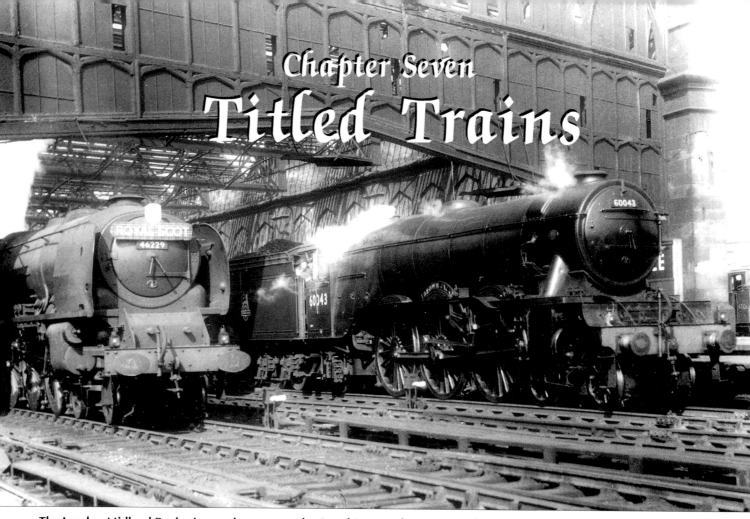

The London Midland Region's premier express, the *Royal Scot* ran between London Euston and Glasgow Central and was the preserve of the Coronations. Upperby crews shared this work between Carlisle and London with Camden men; all were volunteers due the mileage involved, but rewards were handsome. Pay packets were nearly doubled for the two (occasionally three) trips to London per week. No.46229 *Duchess of Hamilton,* suitably adorned with the distinctive tartan headboard, waits to relieve the locomotive on the incoming up working on 28th March 1956. An immaculate Haymarket A3 No.60043 *Brown Jack* has arrived with an express from Edinburgh. *Brown Jack* was the last A3 to be built, whilst *Duchess of Hamilton* still has a sloping smoke-box, a reminder of its former streamliner years. Frank Alcock.

A sun dappled Citadel station on 25th September 1954 hosts a newly built BR 8P Pacific, No.71000 *Duke of Gloucester* in charge of the up *Mid-day Scot.* This Glasgow Central-London Euston express was a Crewe North working and this locomotive, unpopular with crews, was frequently rostered for it. Frank Alcock.

Above. Soon after leaving Citadel station, Coronation No.46221 *Queen Elizabeth* passes the former Caledonian Viaduct yard with the down 'Royal Scot' some time in the mid-fifties. Stephen C. Crook.

Left. Introduced as late as 1957, *The Caledonian* was a short-lived express that linked Euston with Glasgow Central. Carlisle Upperby crews were only involved with this working on the up train each Monday. For the remainder of the week the train in both directions was the preserve of Camden men working as far north as Carlisle. This was the last titled express to be handed over to diesel traction, a reluctant decision based on the fact that the English Electric Type 4 diesels simply could not maintain the schedule. Camden's No.46239 *City of Chester* is seen prior to departure with the up train on 8th September 1959. K. Runton.

The Thames-Clyde Express ran between London St. Pancras and Glasgow St. Enoch using the former G&SWR and the Settle-Carlisle lines. At the time of this photograph in June 1959 the train was worked by one of Holbeck's Royal Scots; one of them, No.46113 *Cameronian,* is coasting towards London Road Junction with the up working. Peter Brock.

Class A4 Pacific No.60009 *Union of South Africa* heads away from Citadel station with the down *Waverley*, about 1962. This express was also routed across the former Midland line to Carlisle, where the usual Holbeck Jubilee was normally replaced by a Haymarket or Canal A3 for the remainder of the journey to Edinburgh. It was very unusual to see an A4 on this working. A respected former Canal driver commented that the reason for working over the Waverley route rather than the usual stamping ground on the east coast main line would be to acquire some final mileage prior to being 'shopped'. J. A. Brown.

Prior to the emergence of the car-owning society, excursion trains to Silloth were a regular feature on summer weekends for the citizens of Carlisle. Canal's Fowler 2-6-4T No.42317 departs Citadel with a Sunday excursion train for Silloth probably during 1961/62. A small number of these powerful locomotives were transferred to the Canal during 1961 to replace the J39 0-6-0s. Peter Brock.

With a variety of semaphore signals on display, Ivatt 2-6-0 No.43141 passes Carlisle No.1 box heading towards Canal Junction with the 6.13pm stopping train to Hawick, during 1959. Stephen C. Crook.

Chapter Eight
Passenger Traffic

A safety valve lifts on Jubilee No.45680 *Camperdown* indicating its readiness for departure with a local passenger working to Hellifield during 1962. This was one of the services Kingmoor used to pass out footplate crews, the frequent stopping being an important element in locomotive and boiler control. K. Armstrong.

Leeds Neville Hill A3 No.60084 *Trigo* waits departure from Carlisle with a northbound express from Leeds to Glasgow St. Enoch. These workings had been the preserve of Holbeck Royal Scots until 1960 when they were ousted by an influx of A3s into the Leeds area. The non-corridor stock in the background forms an afternoon train to Langholm; the Canal Ivatt class 4 2-6-0 in charge would be No.43139, a regular on the service. K. Armstrong.

In addition to the A3 workings over the Midland line from Leeds, A1 Pacifics also began to appear during the early 1960s. Neville Hill's No.60154 *Bon Accord* is seen shortly after arrival with an express at Carlisle in September 1964. G.W. Routledge.

With the advanced repeater signal showing 'off', No.72006 *Clan Mackenzie* departs No.5 bay platform with a Midland line stopping train in April 1965. A class of only ten, they were equally divided between Kingmoor and Polmadie for most of their working lives. Although the ones at Kingmoor survived nearly to the end of the steam era, the five Scottish ones were reported as stored at Polmadie during 1962. This led to Mr. Oliver Rice, the leading fitter at Kingmoor to enquire if they could be 'shopped' at Crewe before being allocated to the Carlisle shed. History shows that the request was unsuccessful as the Polmadie ones proceeded to the scrap-yard. G.W. Routledge.

Jubilee No.45626 *Seychelles* leaves Carlisle past Durranhill Junction (Midland) signal box with the up 1M85 express on 1st August 1964. By now the yards at Durranhill are empty with all of the work transferred to the new marshalling yard at Kingmoor. To further illustrate the decline of the once busy area, the rubble to the left is all that remains of the former Midland steam shed. The Durranhill (NE) signal box can be seen above the second coach of the train. David Forsyth, Paul Chancellor Collection.

Fowler 2-6-4T No.42343 with a stopping train for Hellifield stands next to Canal A3 No.60095 *Flamingo* with a Newcastle express on 24th August 1956. Note the enamel advertisement boards on the station wall. J.L. Stevenson, courtesy Hamish Stevenson.

With London Road yard (NE) visible in the background, Gresley Class V2 No.60969 storms past Durranhill NE signal box on 4th March 1958 with a Carlisle-Newcastle express. An unidentified Fowler tank has been rostered by Upperby to work trip No.68, moving wagons from yard to yard within the city. K. Runton.

Thompson B1 No.61222 stands at the head of a Newcastle express on 29th September 1959. The locomotive is fitted with a Stone generator to power the electric lights, but traditional paraffin lamps are still required during daylight hours to clearly identify the class of train being hauled. David Forsyth, Paul Chancellor collection.

After having cleared London Road Junction, V2 2-6-2 No.60886 heads a down express past the site of the Cowans & Sheldon works before completing the short climb into Citadel station, on 8th August 1964. David Forsyth, Paul Chancellor Collection.

Gateshead V2 No. 60868 has worked a Newcastle to Heads of Ayr train as far as Carlisle on 17th August 1963. Why it is passing No. 4 signal box in what appears to be 'back gear' is somewhat of a mystery as it would be highly improbable that it was proceeding to Upperby shed for servicing. The buildings in the background are former goods sheds in the recently closed Viaduct yard. Peter Fitton.

A classic example of the variety on offer at Carlisle as D34 No.62471 *Glen Falloch,* from Edinburgh St Margarets shed, runs through Citadel station on 26th September 1959. David Forsyth, Paul Chancellor collection.

With the roundhouse at Upperby visible in the distance, Stanier Black Five No.45135 coasts northbound towards the Citadel station with an eleven coach express on 2nd July 1966. David Forsyth, Paul Chancellor Collection.

Britannia No.70034 *Thomas Hardy* storms under St. Nicholas Bridge near Upperby with 1M23, an Edinburgh-Birmingham express. The 5A Crewe North shedplate indicates the period, for 70034 was allocated there for twelve months following June 1964. Stephen C. Crook.

A commendably clean Scottish Region Clan No.72001 *Clan Cameron* passes Upperby yard with an up express in 1961. Although not unknown working south of Carlisle, the Polmadie ones were still something of a rarity to most enthusiasts south of the border city. Former North British 0-6-0 No.65312 is in the background employed on yard to yard transfer duties. Stephen C. Crook.

Polmadie Coronation class No.46230 *Duchess of Buccleuch* passes Upperby at the head of an up express, about 1960. The enginemen's hostel is just visible between the two locomotives. J.A. Brown.

Safety valves lift on grimy Princess Royal No.46205 *Princess Victoria*, at the north end of platform one on 28th July 1960. This was the only member of the original class to be fitted with rocking levers to work the valves of the inside cylinders. Part of one lever can be seen positioned immediately ahead of the outside cylinder steam chest. David Forsyth, Paul Chancellor Collection.

Kingmoor's No.45742 *Connaught* awaits the right away with a local train to Dumfries on 24th July 1963. Peter Fitton.

Jubilees were among the classes prohibited from working south of Crewe after 1st September 1964 due to the energising of further sections of the overhead line. Locomotives had a broad yellow stripe painted on the cab-sides as an indication of the restriction. Holbeck Jubilee No.45697 *Achilles* is so daubed, running into Carlisle Citadel station in June 1966 with a Leeds-Glasgow express. Howard Routledge.

St Margarets A3 No.60077 *The White Knight* backs onto the stock of a Liverpool to Barry Links troop train on 13th June 1964. J. L. Stevenson, courtesy Hamish Stevenson.

Kingmoor's No.46115 *Scots Guardsman* takes water at the north end of platform one at Carlisle with the 1.12pm combined Liverpool/Manchester to Glasgow express on 31st July 1965. This was one of only two of the class in existence at this time; the other, No.46140, was also at Kingmoor. Both were withdrawn from service before the end of that year. Howard Routledge.

Carnforth shed has obviously been hard pressed for power for this northbound express, which has arrived at Carlisle headed by Stanier 8F No.48712. Off picture is a Britannia Pacific which replaced the 8F for the remainder of the journey on 27th May 1966. Howard Routledge.

Kingmoor Coronation No.46255 *City of Hereford* is in the final six weeks of service before withdrawal, but is still charged with a west coast main line express, entering Citadel station on 28th July 1964. David Forsyth, Paul Chancellor collection.

Carnforth Black Five No.45212 restarts 1M32, a Glasgow-Morecambe (SO) summer working on 31st July 1965. These trains, together with those to Blackpool, remained steam hauled until nearly the end of steam in the north-west. Howard Routledge.

A St Margarets D49 4-4-0, No.62733 *Northumberland*, runs north through Citadel station on 1st April 1961. An A3 Pacific stands at the buffer-stops of No.7 bay platform. The D49s were regularly seen on the Waverley route on secondary passenger workings. David Forsyth, Paul Chancellor Collection.

Kingmoor driver Tommy Boothman waits on the right away on V2 No.60931 at Carlisle with a Waverley route passenger train, on 20th February 1965. G.W. Routledge.

The last remaining steam sheds in Scotland had closed by 1st May 1967, but a few remained available to service locomotives that worked over the border after that date. By late July steam was all but extinct in Scotland. Britannia Pacific No.70023 *Venus* leaves Carlisle Citadel with a relief to the 12.30pm Crewe-Glasgow on 26th May 1967. Martin Welch.

Chapter Nine
Goods Lines

Carlisle had a set of goods lines that completely avoided the Citadel station. Diverging from the west coast main line south of Upperby at No.13 box, they ran through Upperby yard and then to the west of the station before running parallel, once again, with the main line as far as Kingmoor yard. With the west coast main line on the extreme right, Canal's J39 No.64895 runs tender first at Upperby with trip No.50 on the down goods, 13th May 1961. R.S. Greenwood.

Having progressed under the footbridge, 64895 heads towards Bog Junction with the yard transfer goods train. Upperby yard has a busy look about it, whilst the shed's antiquated coaling plant is visible in the background. It was to have been replaced when the new roundhouse was built, but the money ran out. R.S. Greenwood.

No.70045 *Lord Rowallan*, shorn of its plates, heads a southbound freight on the up goods line through Upperby yard on 9th July 1966. The lines to the right lead to London Road Junction, giving access to both Newcastle and Settle lines. David Forsyth, Paul Chancellor Collection.

With permissive block working in operation, matters have ground to a halt on the up goods line at Upperby on 2nd July 1966. Black 5 No.45376 has drawn up to the rear of a stationary goods train while 9F No.92012 has been allowed up to the rear of the ever-growing queue awaiting access to the west coast main line. This exact location was the scene of a spectacular collision which is featured in Chapter 11. David Forsyth, Paul Chancellor collection.

Looking north from St. Nicholas Bridge on 2nd July 1966. The freight lines from Upperby begin to run parallel with those from Petteril Bridge Junction. Britannia Pacific No.70009 *Alfred the Great* (name missing) heading a southbound freight towards Upperby, has passed underneath the bridge which used to serve the now derelict Crown Street Goods Depot. David Forsyth, Paul Chancellor Collection.

Both sets of goods lines run parallel for a short distance from St Nicholas Bridge up to Rome Street signal box. Stanier class 5 No.45195 passes Bog Junction signal box on 15th July 1966 with a freight, most probably from the Settle-Carlisle line; the unidentified Ivatt class 4 has come from the Upperby direction. The lines diverging in the bottom right lead to west Cumberland. David Forsyth, Paul Chancellor Collection.

Taken from the same vantage point as the previous photograph but looking north sees Black Five No.44883 heading in the direction of Petteril Bridge Junction with an up freight, on 20th July 1966. Rome Street signal box can be seen above the freight train disappearing under the bridge. David Forsyth, Paul Chancellor Collection.

A former Midland Railway 4F 0-6-0, Kingmoor's No.43953, stands on the goods line opposite Denton Holme Goods Depot on 17th July 1964. Freight trains could also be routed on to the lines next to the goods depot, rejoining the goods line at Denton Holme North signal box. The River Caldew is to the right of the picture. David Forsyth, Paul Chancellor Collection.

Ivatt Class 4 No.43120 runs north past Denton Holme North signal box on 27th August 1965. The lines to the right of the box lead to Denton Holme goods yard. David Forsyth, Paul Chancellor Collection.

Heading south towards Denton Holme North signal box on 19th July 1959, Newton Heath's No.45076 has been borrowed by Upperby to work Trip No.72. The lines in the centre of the picture lead to the Caledonian Viaduct yard whilst those on the extreme right form the west coast main line. Alec Swain, The Transport Treasury.

Class 8F No.48542 is crossing the River Eden with a down freight to the marshalling yard at Kingmoor on 4th June 1965. The photograph, which was taken from the Caledonian Bridge, gives a good view of the trackwork to the north of the city. The sidings on the right were operated by the since-demolished power station. Martin Welch.

46244 *King George V1* heads from the down goods line to cross Etterby Junction in order to gain access to its home at Kingmoor on 1st July 1964. The locomotive is on the newer bridge of the two, built in 1942; it was a wartime necessity to deal with the increase in freight traffic moving through the city at that time. David Forsyth, Paul Chancellor collection.

Britannia No.70045 *Lord Rowallan* uses the well trodden path which connects the down goods line with the entry to Kingmoor shed at Etterby Junction on 2nd July 1966. The date on the bridge is a reminder of the wartime doubling of the tracks over the River Eden. Howard Routledge.

The 4F 0-6-0s had been familiar in Carlisle over many decades but at the time of this photograph, August 1965, the last ones allocated to the city had been withdrawn from traffic for some time. It therefore came as quite a surprise to see No.44086 emerge from under the Caledonian Bridge with a freight from west Cumberland to Kingmoor Yard. Howard Routledge.

A view northwards from the Caledonian Bridge on 25th March 1967 sees 8F No.48151 at the beginning of her journey shortly after leaving the Kingmoor marshalling yard. The engine has the odd bits of cleaning and painting that appeared around this time, as well as the re-arranged lamp irons. To counter the possibility of electrocution as the top lamp was put on, the iron was lowered to the smokebox door, as shown here. The middle one on the buffer beam was also altered, so that it was aligned with the new 'top' iron. Kingmoor steam shed, which has only a further nine months existence, is totally obscured by the smoke, as the new diesel depot begins to take shape. David Forsyth, Paul Chancellor Collection.

Designed to eliminate the seven pre-grouping yards within Carlisle, the new marshalling yard at Kingmoor nears completion on 30th May 1962. Built at a price of £5m, the yard was believed to be the largest in Europe. With 70 miles of track including 150 sidings, it was designed to handle 5,000 wagons daily. This view, looking north, shows the down reception sidings; the west coast main line is on the right. The building is 'the F & I', the fuelling and inspection shed for diesels. K. Runton.

Stanier 4-6-0 No.44795 runs tender first past the Kingmoor power box and into the new yard with the Kingmoor Cowans and Sheldon 75 ton steam crane, about 1966. G. Hamsher.

Single chimney A2 No.60535 *Hornet's Beauty* heads a Carlisle to Glasgow freight towards Floriston. The goods lines, on either side of the west coast main lines, were originally loops which stretched from Rockcliffe to Floriston but they were converted to connect with the new marshalling yard at Kingmoor. The up goods line can be seen climbing to cross the main lines via the flyover bridge seen in the distance, near to Rockcliffe station. Bill Ashcroft.

Freight trains from Kingmoor to Millerhill had to be pulled tender first out of the marshalling yard to a loop at Stainton on the Waverley line whereupon the locomotive detached before running round to couple to the front of the train. Gresley V2 No.60835 re-starts a down freight at Stainton in August 1965. Howard Routledge.

By the time this photograph was taken, the first station out of Carlisle on the line to Newcastle was Wetheral, where we see Ivatt Class 4 No.43023 with a pick-up goods on 12th August 1964. Persons using the footbridge are oblivious to the efforts of railway staff, struggling with a large cable drum in the wagon under the bridge. David Forsyth, Paul Chancellor Collection.

A photograph full of detail shows 9F No.92249 running onto Kingmoor shed on 12th June 1965. Kingmoor received its first 9Fs in June 1964 when six arrived to work the heavy Hardendale limestone trains forward from Kingmoor yard to the Ravenscraig steelworks near Motherwell. Martin Welch.

A classic view of Peppercorn A2 Pacific No.60532 *Blue Peter,* at Kingmoor in October 1966, clearly showing the modifications made during 1949 when a double chimney and multiple valve regulator were fitted. It is difficult to comprehend that this locomotive, built in 1948, was withdrawn from service within two months of this photograph being taken. David S. Goodfellow.

Kingmoor close-ups on 30th January 1966, showing the different types of smoke deflectors fitted to the Britannias. After the serious derailment of No.70026 *Polar Star* in 1955 it was suggested that the conventional handrail on the smoke deflector may have impaired the view of the driver. Consequently, handrails were modified on some engines but it was not taken wholly seriously and others retained the original handrails to the end. Here we have original rails on *Firth of Tay*, the round hand holds fitted at Crewe and the rectangular cut-outs favoured by Swindon. Howard Routledge.

Chapter Eleven
Accidents

The west coast main line near Plumpton, north of Penrith, became completely blocked during the early hours of 8th May 1954 as a result of a derailment involving nineteen vehicles of a Warrington to Carlisle freight. The locomotive and six leading wagons were undamaged. The cause of the incident was believed to be a 'hot box'. Stanier Class 5 No.45439 and breakdown cranes are in evidence as workmen remove the wreckage in order to get the lines re-opened. The BR road vehicle will be of interest to some whilst the local police appear to have travelled to the scene on motor cycles.
Frank Alcock.

Two views of another Warrington to Carlisle freight derailment, this time involving 4-6-0 No.45197 which has overturned and become embedded in soft earth beside the main line south of Penrith. For whatever the reason, the train has obviously approached the end of the long down loop too fast and failed to comply with the 15mph speed restriction imposed there. The Kingmoor breakdown crane is lifting one of the wagons whilst packing, in the form of wooden sleepers, have been placed near to the locomotive in readiness for the recovery work. E. Devaney.

Whilst the England football team were winning the World Cup at Wembley on 30th July 1966, Britannia No.70017 *Arrow* was also making the headlines as a result of a spectacular collision on Carlisle's goods line near to Upperby yard. Heading the 11.45am Polmadie-Morecambe empty stock, it ran into the rear of a stationary 3.20pm Carlisle-Liverpool freight. The goods lines from Carlisle No.13 box (south of Upperby) to Kingmoor yard were worked under permissive block regulations meaning that more than one train was allowed into a section at a given time. Such a practice obviously required keen observation by footplate staff. Miraculously no-one was seriously hurt but the locomotive was condemned as a result of the incident. Peter Brock.

The aftermath of a serious collision which occurred at Little Salkeld on the Settle-Carlisle line on 22nd August 1961 when a double headed freight ran into a previous derailment. The two Kingmoor locomotives, Fowler class 4F 0-6-0 No.44181 and Ivatt class 4 No.43023, had been running tender to tender when confronted with the obstruction. J.A.Brown.

An investigation will no doubt take place to determine how Jubilee No.45588 *Kashmir* has ran tender first into the turntable pit at Upperby. One theory could be that the locking pin wasn't secured into the wall before the locomotive moved onto the 'table. Water is being pumped out of the tender in order to reduce weight prior to recovery taking place. The shed staff must be thankful that the incident didn't occur on the turntable inside the roundhouse. G.W. Routledge collection.

A view of the Viaduct yard, circa 1960, showing the aftermath of a serious derailment involving petroleum tankers. The incident has completely blocked the entry/exit to the yard. Derek Glover.

Chapter Twelve
The Last Silloth Train

The Beeching report deemed the Carlisle to Silloth branch uneconomic and it was duly listed for closure. The final train ran on 6th September 1964 and was entrusted to steam haulage. Ivatt Class 4 No.43139 was selected to carry out the honours with former Canal driver Jimmy Lister at the controls. Large crowds, as these pages reveal, gathered to witness the event and the railway police under the command of Inspector Greenwood had their hands full in keeping the tracks clear before the arrival of the train. When the train eventually arrived it was near nightfall. With the turntable not having seen regular use for some time, the crew had decided not to risk using it and had ran the first leg tender first. G.W. Routledge.

Black Five No.45380 storms through Cumwhinton on the 1 in 132 climb out of Carlisle with an up freight on 3rd July 1964. A typical Midland rural station, Cumwhinton had been closed during 1958 and for some years after that was used by a tyre salvage company. David Forsyth, Paul Chancellor Collection.

Kingmoor Clan No.72006 *Clan Mackenzie* with a lightweight three coach stopping train near Cotehill, some six miles south of Carlisle, about 1965. J.A. Brown.

Heaton Mersey 8F No.48684 heads an up freight towards Armathwaite Tunnel on 3rd June 1966. The fireman appears to have a good fire, and with steam feathering at the safety valves, he (or maybe the chap is some lucky civilian getting a footplate ride…) can take time to enjoy the views offered by the Eden valley. David S. Goodfellow.

Skipton BR Class 4 No.75041 pilots 8F No.48474 up the final approach to Ais Gill summit with a class 8 unfitted freight on 16th September 1966. It was unusual for freights to be double-headed on the former Midland line. One explanation for the pilot could be that the Standard was working back to its home shed; put on the freight it would have saved signalling sections being occupied by only a light engine movement. David S. Goodfellow.

The big freeze of 1963 brought havoc to the railway network. Both the Waverley route and the Settle-Carlisle line were closed for some time after snow-plough crews had been defeated by the depth of drifts in the more exposed areas. Without a rail in sight and with snow still falling, these hardy Kingmoor souls have somehow reached Ais Gill summit with a 4F 0-6-0, No.44009, piloting an unidentified WD 2-8-0. Their mission was to recover an abandoned double-headed snow-plough unit which had

Jubilee No. 45584 *North West Frontier* near Wreay with a Carlisle-Manchester stopping train in July 1964. The locomotive has received the attention of an unofficial band of cleaners, which included the photographer and two of his friends. Stephen C. Crook.

An up freight climbs through the closed Wreay station in August 1961 behind Upperby Patriot No.45507 *Royal Tank Corps*. Stephen C. Crook.

The first set of loops south of Carlisle on the west coast main line were at Southwaite from where Black Five No.44780 is re-starting an up freight, on 26th May 1967. Martin Welch.

Carlisle Kingmoor Black Five No.45012 runs through Penrith with an up freight, about 1966. Although faced with a stiff climb to Shap summit, the fireman appears to be taking thing easy, apparently unaware that an injector has 'knocked off'. G. Hamsher.

No.72009 *Clan Stewart* takes water at Penrith whilst in charge of an up goods in November 1964. Partially obscured by steam, the fireman can just be seen on the tender top releasing water from the holding tank by 'pulling the chain'. The station name board on the opposite platform will evoke memories of a more complete rail system than that of today. G.W. Routledge.

'Britannia' No.70041 *Sir John Moore* runs tender first south of Penrith with empties for Hardendale Quarry at Shap in November 1964. The line in the background led to Keswick. G.W. Routledge.

A typically grimy Kingmoor Jubilee, No.45613 *Kenya,* passes Penrith No.1 signal box with an up freight in June 1963. Stephen C. Crook.

Patriot No.45529 *Stephenson* has received a heavy round of firing in preparation for the climb to Shap summit as it passes Eamont Junction, south of Penrith, with a class 5 freight in June 1963. Upperby Royal Scot No.46136 *The Border Regiment* stands at signals on the down loop. Stephen C. Crook.

Six miles south of Penrith and immaculate Jubilee No.45599 *Bechuanaland* from Nuneaton shed, is climbing hard at 1 in 125 near to Strickland Wood with an up fitted freight on 4th August 1962. Peter Fitton.

Black Five No.45148 appears well prepared for the final few miles climb to Shap summit as it passes Thrimby Grange signal box with a Glasgow-Liverpool express on 31st July 1965. Peter Fitton.

No.45584 *North West Frontier* rushes down from the summit and through a rain-soaked Shap station with a Blackpool Central to Perth express on 18th July 1964. It is worth noting the efforts of the photographer who had spent the previous day at Blackpool Central shed cleaning the locomotive, only to be thwarted by the summer weather so typical in the northern fells. Peter Fitton.

Britannia No.70038 *Robin Hood* sweeps across Shap summit on 22nd July 1967 with 1M38, the 2pm Glasgow to Liverpool express. The new blue and white liveried coaching stock is evident in the train. Peter Fitton.

The name 'Shap' will always conjure up memories of the banking engines that were employed to push heavy northbound trains up the 1 in 75 incline from Tebay to Shap summit. The 1960s saw Fowler, Fairburn and Stanier 2-6-4Ts on the work before being replaced during the last days of steam by BR 4MT 4-6-0s. Fairburn No.42252 begins the final push up to the summit as it leaves the open expanse of Shap Wells on 8th March 1967. Note the storm sheet fitted above the cab door to counteract the westerly winds. David S. Goodfellow.

With the sound of a slow unassisted climb reverberating across the Westmorland fells, the driver of 8F No.48491 has decided to 'go for it' without the aid of a banker for the ascent to Shap summit on 20th December 1967. Kingmoor and Tebay sheds had only ten days left before closure, an event which consigned sights like this to the history books. Peter Fitton.

The expansive qualities of steam are amply demonstrated in the cold air surrounding Shap Wells on 20th December 1967 as Britannia No.70024 *Vulcan* toils up Shap bank assisted at the rear by Standard 4MT No.75030. By the end of the following week this striking ritual was over for good. Peter Fitton.

A heavy Crewe to Carlisle parcels train double-headed by Black 5s Nos. 44878 and 44674, climbing past Shap Wells on 8th March 1967. As on most days, the weather front is from the west but on this particular day the wind appears near gale force as the exhaust from both locomotives lies virtually horizontal across the fell-side. David S. Goodfellow.

Stanier class 5 No.44697, with self-weighing tender, storms past the tiny Scout Green signal box with a lightweight 1L13 Manchester to Keswick express on 15th August 1964. Peter Fitton.

A commendably clean Royal Scot No.46115 *Scots Guardsman* has the assistance of a banking engine as it climbs through Greenholme with a fitted freight on 3rd June 1965. The external condition of the locomotive, together with the nameplates restored, could be attributed to a recent society special. Martin Welch.

Above. For those northbound trains requiring a helping hand up both Grayrigg and Shap banks, the assisting locomotive was coupled in front of the train engine at Oxenholme. On 13th September 1966 Stanier 2-6-4T No.42665 pilots Carnforth Black Five No.44905 past Tebay shed, ready for the climb to the summit. Howard Routledge.

Right. Seen from Tebay No.2 signal box, Fowler 2-6-4T No.42414 pilots Jubilee No.45598 *Basutoland* through Tebay with the 1S99 Blackpool Central to Glasgow relief on 15th August 1964. Peter Fitton.

Chapter Fifteen

Specials Gallery

In the final years of steam, charter trains organised by railway societies began appearing in Carlisle, no doubt enticed by the climbs of Shap, Beattock, Whitrope and Ais Gill. Other than the appearance of 46225 on the 1956 test trains, the first occasion that a Coronation traversed the Settle-Carlisle line in revenue service was on 9th July 1961 when 46247 *City of Liverpool* hauled a charter for the Railway Correspondence and Travel Society from Leeds to Carlisle. The train is approaching the outskirts of Carlisle passing Durranhill south sidings. J.A. Brown.

Left. The British Gypsum Cocklakes works was south of Carlisle at Cotehill, the complex being connected to the former Midland line at Howe & Co's signal box. The annual children's outing has obviously given the company joiner some work with a difference in producing this magnificent headboard to mark the 1962 event. No.72007 *Clan Mackintosh* gets into its stride as it heads north passing Kingmoor en-route to Ayr. J.A. Brown.

Middle. Carlisle Canal resident A3 No.60093 *Coronach* passes Durranhill NE signal box with a special train conveying supporters of Carlisle United to an FA Cup-tie at Darlington in November 1961. The photograph was taken by the signalman ably assisted by fireman Peter Brock; the photographic work of both of them features elsewhere in this book. K. Runton.

One of the most enterprising rail-tours to visit Carlisle was the 'Solway Ranger' on 13th June 1964. Organised by the Railway Correspondence and Travel Society (RCTS), it featured a Southern Region Merchant Navy Pacific and two of the Scottish veterans, former GNSR No.49 *Gordon Highlander* and Caledonian Railway No.123. The pair are first seen shortly after departure from Citadel station (below), both drivers having shut the regulators in order to drift down to Port Carlisle Junction where they will take the line to Canal Junction and then onto the Silloth branch (opposite). Peter Fitton.

In what surely must be a first, No.123 runs on to the turntable at Silloth. Introduced in 1886, the locomotive was withdrawn in 1935 but was returned to service in 1958 for special use. Peter Fitton.

Whilst the Scottish oldsters visited Silloth, Nine Elms Merchant Navy No.35012 *United States Lines* was serviced at Kingmoor; here it is positioned for turning prior to running down to Citadel station from where it will take the train back south. Peter Fitton.

The instruction was issued to withdraw from service the last remaining Coronations by 13th September 1964, but the RCTS already had an agreement in place with the London Midland Region to have No.46256 *Sir William A. Stanier F.R.S* on a tour to run on the 26th of that same month. Titled the 'Scottish Lowlander', the train ran from Crewe to Carlisle (46256) on to Edinburgh (A4 No.60007) and then Edinburgh to Glasgow and back to Carlisle with A4 No.60009 *Union of South Africa*. No.60009 has arrived at Citadel station while the sole surviving Coronation, No.46256, waits to return the train to Crewe. Upon its arrival on Crewe North shed, the locomotive was immediately withdrawn from service to await its fate in a Staffordshire scrapyard. Howard Malham.

The 'Rebuilt Scot Tour' was another RCTS charter, which ran from Crewe to Carlisle and return on 13th February 1965. The route outward was via the Settle-Carlisle line and the return via Shap. The locomotive initially selected by Bill Ashcroft of the RCTS was No.46160, chosen for the good condition of its paintwork when seen at Crewe in late 1964. At the last minute, Kingmoor decided to provide No.46115, considered to be in a better mechanical condition. No. 46115 *Scots Guardsman* is getting into her stride passing Upperby with the returning charter. The footbridge spanning the tracks will evoke a lot memories for scores of local enthusiasts, for it was the preferred route into the shed for non-permit holders! Peter Fitton.

Citadel station on 3rd September 1966, and members of the South West Railway Society view the changeover of locomotives involved in the 'Granite City' charter from Euston to Aberdeen. The train had arrived behind Upperby Britannia No.70032 *Tennyson* which was replaced by V2 No.60836 for the run over the Waverley route. It is believed that this was the last occasion a V2 visited the city. Howard Routledge.

Class A2 Pacific No.60532 *Blue Peter* is a long way from its home at Dundee after working a special from Edinburgh to Carlisle via the Waverley route on 8th October 1966. A Black 5 waits the passage of the Pacific before it can proceed from the confines of Kingmoor shed. David S. Goodfellow.

Already in private ownership but retaining its British Railways identity, A4 No.60019 *Bittern* heads towards Port Carlisle Junction on 12th November 1966 with a re-run of the 'Waverley', organised by the A4 Locomotive Society. Howard Routledge.

A charter arranged by the Locomotive Club of Great Britain ran on 4th June 1966 in atrocious weather conditions. Double-headed by Jubilees 45593 *Kolhapur* and 45596 *Bahamas*, the train is approximately one mile south of Durranhill approaching Scotby on the former Midland line. The former NER line to Newcastle is on the extreme right. Martin Welch.

Farnley Junction's 45562 *Alberta* makes an unusual appearance at Brampton Junction on the Carlisle-Newcastle line with the 'Thames-Tyne Limited' on 3rd June 1967. Martin Welch.

45697 *Achilles* enters Citadel station on 11th December 1965 with a Warwickshire Railway Society railtour from Leeds to Edinburgh. *Achilles* was replaced by A2 60528 *Tudor Minstrel* for the run over the Waverley route. Howard Routledge.

Restored to LNER apple green livery and sporting a single chimney, 4472 *Flying Scotsman* re-starts another WRS charter from Kingmoor on 4th September 1965. Howard Routledge.

The Stephenson Locomotive Society ran the Pennine Summits railtour on 12th July 1964. Coronation No.46251 *City of Nottingham* had brought the train north over Shap straight onto the up loop at Kingmoor allowing passengers the opportunity to visit the depot. 46255 *City of Hereford* waits to return the train south via the Settle-Carlisle line. Alec Swain, The Transport Treasury.